Helen Keller

Steve Young

Benjamin Franklin

8 STEPS *to* LASTING EXCELLENCE

CAMERON C. TAYLOR

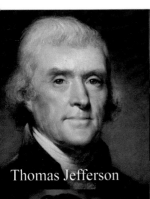
Thomas Jefferson

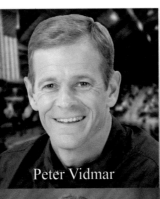
Peter Vidmar

Joan of Arc

Philo Farnsworth

Martin Luther King Jr.

Lou Holtz

Other Books by Cameron C. Taylor

8 Attributes of Great Achievers

8 Attributes of Great Achievers, Volume II

Preserve, Protect, & Defend

Does Your Bag Have Holes? 24 Truths That Lead to Financial and Spiritual Freedom

Twelve Paradoxes of the Gospel

Author Website

www.CameronCTaylor.com

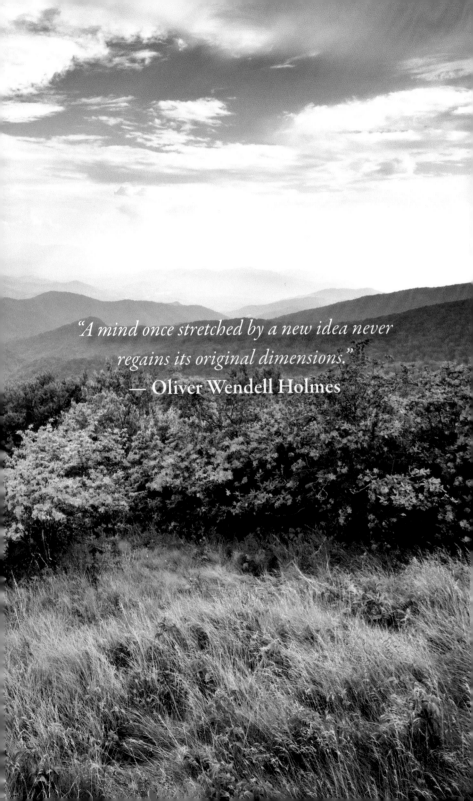

"A mind once stretched by a new idea never regains its original dimensions."
— Oliver Wendell Holmes

Table of Contents

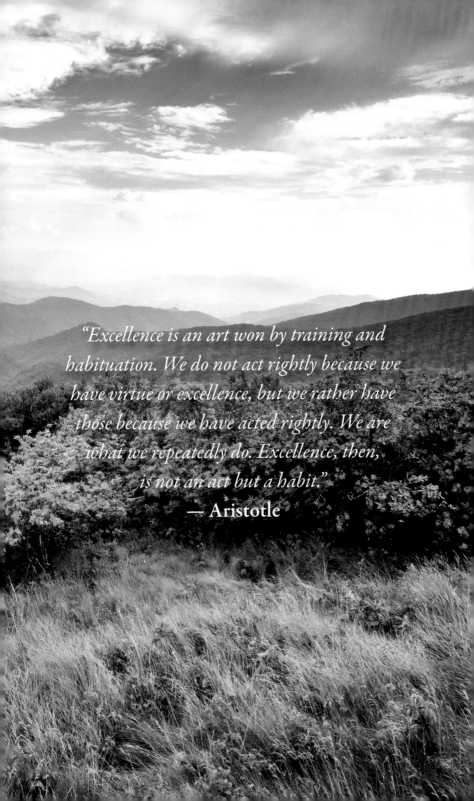

"Excellence is an art won by training and habituation. We do not act rightly because we have virtue or excellence, but we rather have those because we have acted rightly. We are what we repeatedly do. Excellence, then, is not an act but a habit."

— **Aristotle**

WHAT PRODUCES LASTING EXCELLENCE?

"Learning is an incremental process. No matter what the subject, you must first learn the fundamentals, putting in long hours to master the basics.... All talented individuals develop their talents over long periods of time."
— Lou Holtz

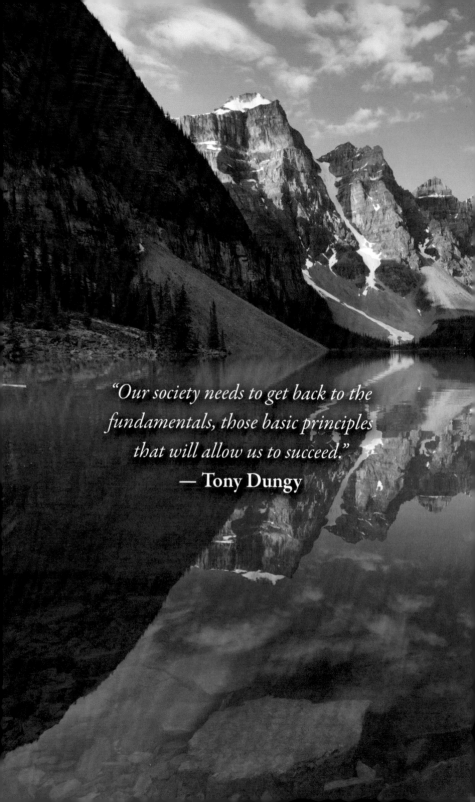

"Our society needs to get back to the fundamentals, those basic principles that will allow us to succeed."
— Tony Dungy

WHAT PRODUCES LASTING EXCELLENCE?

The author of the book *Good to Great* conducted an extensive five-year research project to identify the factors that produced lasting excellence in companies. One of the critical factors identified was the concept he calls the flywheel. Jim Collins wrote, "Picture a huge heavy flywheel—a massive metal disk mounted horizontally on an axle, about 30 feet in diameter, 2 feet thick, and weighing about 5,000 pounds. Now imagine that your task is to get this flywheel rotating on the axle as fast and as long as possible.... The flywheel image captures the overall feel of what it was like inside the companies as they went from good to great. No matter how dramatic the end result, the good-to-great transformation never happened in one fell swoop. There was no single defining action, no grand program, no one killer innovation. Good to great comes about by the cumulative processes—step by step, action by action, decision by decision, turn by turn of the flywheel...with persistent pushing in a consistent direction over a long period of time...that adds up to sustained and spectacular results."[1] Coach John Wooden wrote, "It takes time to create excellence. If it could be done quickly more people would do it."[2]

The Power of Fundamentals

For over a decade now I have been the keynote speaker at a leadership training conference for high school sophomores on the topic of goal setting. A handful of these students are selected to return the following year to assist at the conference as staff. One of these staff members shared with me the numerous accomplishments he had achieved during the year as he implemented the goal-setting principles I had taught him. His parents, teachers, and classmates noticed the change in him and began asking what he was doing differently that led to his many achievements.

He responded to their questions by stating that he had simply begun to write down his goals and then would work to achieve them. Most of his inquirers were quite surprised by his uncomplicated formula. Goal setting is a simple, fundamental process that produces a dramatic increase in what you can accomplish, yet 97 percent of people do not do it. Studies have found that only 3 percent of Americans have written goals.

Coach Chuck Noll taught, "Champions are champions not because they do anything extraordinary but because they do the ordinary things better than anyone else."[3] It is the small and simple tasks that produce the greatest results.

Just as there are principles that govern nature, such as gravity, there are also principles that govern our happiness, peace, and prosperity. It is by learning and living these principles of success that we experience true success and joy.

Over the years I have built several successful businesses and, with this success, people have often inquired how they too can achieve what I am achieving. I remember on one such occasion, after sharing my simple success principles, my interrogator became livid with me and bellowed, "If you don't want to tell me your secret, just say so," and then marched away. Too often we look for a magical secret or new technique that will produce tremendous returns and results with little effort on our part. Those seeking this kind of secret will never find it—for the secret to success is to continually live and apply basic, simple fundamentals over a long period of time.

"*Playing a tournament is almost an anticlimax. Tournaments are won and lost in preparation. Playing them is just going through the motions.*"
— Ben Hogan, Professional Golfer

8 STEPS TO LASTING EXCELLENCE

"Happiness depends more upon the internal frame of a person's mind than on the externals in the world."
— George Washington

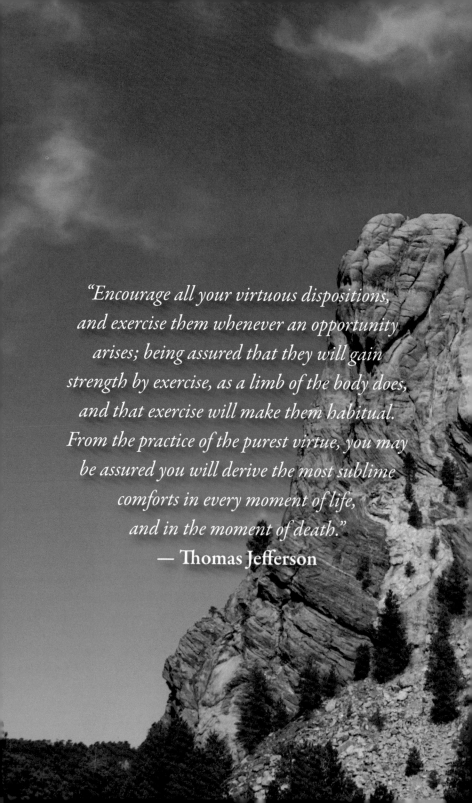

"Encourage all your virtuous dispositions, and exercise them whenever an opportunity arises; being assured that they will gain strength by exercise, as a limb of the body does, and that exercise will make them habitual. From the practice of the purest virtue, you may be assured you will derive the most sublime comforts in every moment of life, and in the moment of death."
— **Thomas Jefferson**

8 STEPS TO
LASTING EXCELLENCE

Lasting excellence is the result of a process, not a single action or event. I have never learned a principle, developed a skill, lost weight, or gained muscle in an instant. Children follow the process of learning to crawl before they walk, and learning to walk before they run. Concert pianists start out learning to play "Chopsticks" and "Mary Had a Little Lamb." After years of practice and effort, they develop their skills to a point that they can play *Beethoven's Fifth Symphony* or Bach's concertos. Excellence takes time. How do we go from where we are to where we want to be? We get there in steps.

Step 1: Define Your Values

Step 2: Discover Your Missions

Step 3: Create Your Vision

Step 4: Write Down Your Goals

Step 5: Read Your Goals Daily

Step 6: Visualize

Step 7: Create an Action Plan

Step 8: Persistence

"If someone makes the greatest chocolate cake in the world, can you produce the same quality results? Of course you can, if you have the person's recipe. A recipe is nothing but a strategy, a specific plan of what resources to use and how to use them to produce a specific result.... So what do you need to produce the same quality cake as the expert baker? You need the recipe, and you need to follow it explicitly. If you follow the recipe to the letter, you will produce the same results, even though you may never have baked such a cake before in your life. The baker may have worked through years of trial and error before finally developing the ultimate recipe. You can save years by following his recipe, by modeling what he did.... If you find people who already have financial success or fulfilling relationships, you just have to discover their strategy and apply it to produce similar results and save tremendous amounts of time and effort."[4]

This book provides the 8-step recipe for success and the activities to execute these steps. Living the 8 steps that produce lasting excellence is done by creating what is called a Statement of Excellence. Creating a Statement of Excellence enables you to learn, apply, and live the principles of success. A Statement of Excellence includes four key elements: values statements, mission statements, a vision statement, and goals.

A Statement of Excellence is a system which enables you to make your ideal a reality and enables ordinary people to accomplish extraordinary things. Mahatma Gandhi taught, "I claim to be no more than an average man with below average capabilities. I have not the shadow of a doubt that any man or woman can achieve what I have if he or she would put forth the same effort and cultivate the same hope and faith." The seeds of greatness are within you. The only thing that stands between where you are and where you want to be is time and effort.

When you are building a house, does the house usually turn out like the blueprint? Of course it does. If you design a house to be 1,000 square feet, the house should be 1,000 square feet when you finish. Before building a house, you first ask yourself, "What kind of house would I like?" The house is first created in elaborate detail on paper before the first piece is set into place. We should use this same process in our lives. "What kind of a life do you want? What do you want to accomplish?" Creating a Statement of Excellence will create a blueprint for your life that you can follow to build the life you desire.

"Everyone who got where he is has had to begin where he was."
— Robert Louis Stevenson

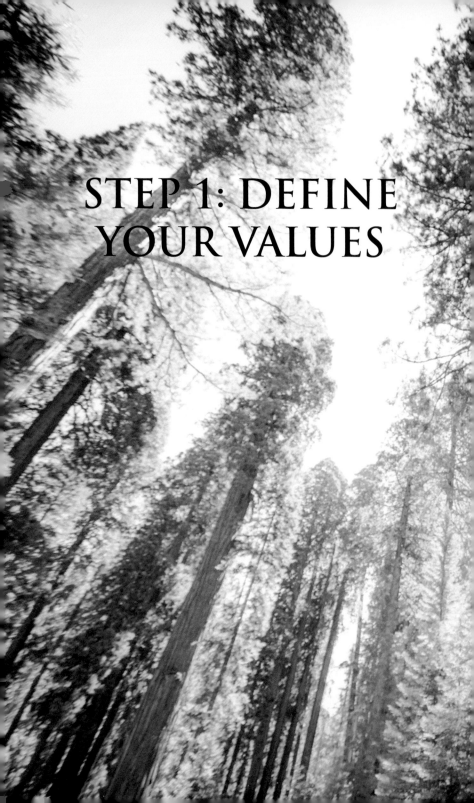

STEP 1: DEFINE
YOUR VALUES

"*Without virtue man can have no happiness in this world.... There was never yet a truly great man that was not at the same time truly virtuous.*"
— **Benjamin Franklin**

"Virtue is not hereditary."
— Thomas Jefferson

STEP 1
DEFINE YOUR VALUES

A values statement describes the principles by which you want to live. Establishing and committing to a set of values is key to living in accordance with principles that bring about lasting excellence and enduring happiness. Creating a values statement helps with decision making. Now is the best time to decide how you are going to live. Making the decision before the situation arises helps us make the correct choices when the pressures of the moment arise. "When your values are clear to you, making decisions becomes easier."[5]

A values statement helps keep what matters most as a priority and guards against your values being pushed aside in daily pursuits. A dear friend and business associate of mine, G. Kent Mangelson, shared with me the following: "After nearly thirty years in the financial business and having associated with thousands of wealthy individuals, I have developed a firm philosophy about people and money. If an individual does not clearly establish personal values and goals before making financial goals, then wealth and the accumulation thereof will begin to take on a life of its own. Without clearly established values to keep the individual's direction in focus, money tends to distract the person, gradually moving them away from everything in life that means the most to them. Sadly and all too often, when it is too late to repair the damage, the person discovers that they have lost those things that meant the most to them and that all the money in the world cannot buy or replace that which is gone."

Benjamin Franklin's Values Statement

A great example of writing and using a values statement is found in the life of Benjamin Franklin. He recorded in his autobiography the desire to live as would please God and wrote down thirteen virtues he wished to possess. They are as follows:

1. TEMPERANCE. Eat not to dullness; drink not to elevation.
2. SILENCE. Speak not but what may benefit others or yourself; avoid trifling conversation.
3. ORDER. Let all your things have their places; let each part of your business have its time.
4. RESOLUTION. Resolve to perform what you ought; perform without fail what you resolve.
5. FRUGALITY. Make no expense but to do good to others or yourself; i.e., waste nothing.
6. INDUSTRY. Lose no time; be always employed in something useful; cut off all unnecessary actions.
7. SINCERITY. Use no hurtful deceit; think innocently and justly, and, if you speak, speak accordingly.

8. JUSTICE. Wrong none by doing injuries, or omitting the benefits that are your duty.

9. MODERATION. Avoid extremes; forbear resenting injuries so much as you think they deserve.

10. CLEANLINESS. Tolerate no uncleanliness in body, clothes, or habitation.

11. TRANQUILITY. Be not disturbed at trifles, or at accidents common or unavoidable.

12. CHASTITY. Rarely use venery but for health or offspring, never to dullness, weakness, or the injury of your own or another's peace or reputation.

13. HUMILITY. Imitate Jesus and Socrates.

Values Statement Examples

Responsible: The story of my life is not written by what happens to me, but by what I choose.

Integrity: I will live by moral and ethical principles and honor my commitments. My word is my bond and a sacred treasure. I will be honest in all my dealings.

Industrious: I will create and serve to make the world a better place. I will exert great effort to produce and accomplish.

Independent: I will do the right thing without being told.

Humble: I will be teachable and continually seek learning.

Optimistic: I will see and expect goodness.

Persistent: Success is a process. I will try until I succeed.

Courageous: I will act even in the face of difficulty and pain.

Grateful: I will recognize and express appreciation for the assistance and kindness I receive.

Servant Leader: I will put the needs of others first and help others develop and perform to their maximum potential.

Faith: I will live a life of faith. I will strive to be an instrument in the hands of God.

Thrifty: I will be a wise steward of the possessions God gives me.

Love: Love will be the foundation upon which my decisions are based. I will use my resources to bless and serve those in need.

Innovator: I will look for ways to improve the lives of others in my family, my community, my nation, and the world.

Boy Scouts of America Values Statement

On my honor I will do my best
to do my duty to God and my country
and to obey the Scout Law;
to help other people at all times;
to keep myself physically strong,
mentally awake, and morally straight.

A scout is trustworthy, loyal, helpful, friendly, courteous, kind, obedient, cheerful, thrifty, brave, clean, and reverent.

Questions to Develop Your Values Statement

On a piece of paper or a computer, answer the following questions and then formulate a rough draft of your values statement.

Write down the four people you most admire and respect and the four attributes you would use to describe them. The attributes that appear will help you identify what you want as your core values.

Person 1. _____
   Attribute   1._____ 2._____
              3._____ 4._____

Person 2. _____
   Attribute   1._____ 2._____
              3._____ 4._____

Person 3. _____
   Attribute   1._____ 2._____
              3._____ 4._____

Person 4. _____
   Attribute   1._____ 2._____
              3._____ 4._____

What principles do I want to live by? (i.e., forgiveness, golden rule, etc.)

What attributes do I desire to possess and exhibit? (i.e., charitable, humble, thrifty, responsible, industrious, honest, virtuous, etc.)

How would I like others to describe me? Who would I like to become?

"*Character may be manifested in the great moments, but it is made in the small ones.*"
— **Phillips Brooks**

STEP 2: DISCOVER YOUR MISSIONS

*"He who has a why to live for
can bear almost any how."*
— **Friedrich Nietzsche**

"God gives us an intrinsic desire to contribute,
add value, and connect with others in some
meaningful endeavor. Finding meaning and
purpose in our work is the key to both personal
fulfillment and professional success."
— Larry Julian

STEP 2
DISCOVER YOUR MISSIONS

We each have various roles/stewardships and responsibilities. I, for example, am the president of multiple organizations, an author, a teacher, a minister, a husband, and a father. Within each of these stewardships, I have a mission and specific goals related to each. Identifying your mission and goals in each stewardship will help you maintain a balance and will help you focus on what is most important.

For Christopher Columbus, one of his missions was to discover new lands. For George Washington, one of his missions was to create a free nation. For Phil Farnsworth, one of his missions was to make the world a better place through invention and innovation. Walt Disney's mission statement for Disneyland was "to make people happy."

The co-founder of Microsoft, Paul Allen, discovered his mission while in high school. He spent many hours in the computer lab and found that he had a great love for programming. He wrote, "Crafting my own computer code felt more creative than anything I'd tried before.... Soon I was spending every lunchtime and free period around the Teletype.... I had discovered my calling. I was a programmer."[6]

As Sam Walton, the founder of Walmart, neared the end of his life dying of cancer, he reflected on his life's work and wondered if he should have spent his time on something else to improve the world. He wondered if he made the right choice to invest so much time in building Walmart. After much thought, he concluded that his work at Walmart was a part of his ministry—that through his retail business, he was able to improve and bless the lives of many others. He wrote, "Preachers are put here to minister to our souls; doctors to heal our diseases; teachers to open up our minds; and so on. Everybody has their role to play." Walton's mission statement for Walmart was to provide a better shopping experience for everyday people living in small towns and to improve their standard of living by providing quality goods at low prices in a pleasant shopping environment.[7]

Discovering Your Missions

"I am not afraid; I was born to do this."
— Joan of Arc

Every individual has a purpose and a mission in life. Viktor Frankl observed, "Everyone has his own specific vocation or mission in life to carry out a concrete assignment which demands fulfillment. Therein he cannot be replaced, nor can his life be repeated. Thus, everyone's task is as unique as is his specific opportunity to implement it."[8]

Dr. Stephen R. Covey echoed this sentiment when he stated, "We detect rather than invent our missions in life.... I think each of us has an internal monitor or sense, a conscience that gives us an awareness of our uniqueness and the singular contributions that we can make." He continued, "Writing...a mission statement changes you because it forces you to think through your priorities deeply, carefully, and to align your behavior with your beliefs. As you do, other people begin to sense that you're not being driven by everything that happens to you. You have a sense of mission about what you're trying to do, and you are excited about it."[9]

"I believe it is well within the natural order of things to have everybody humming while they work. As a noted economist recently stated, 'Unemployment is a characteristic unique to the human species only. All the other creatures and creations seem to know what they are supposed to be doing.'"[10] Identifying your roles/stewardships and your mission within each of these roles gives you a clear answer to the question, "What is my purpose in life and what am I supposed to be doing?" and ensures you maintain focus on what matters most.

Renewal

There is one stewardship that everyone has—personal renewal and growth. Renewal and growth do not happen automatically, so we must continually develop and renew our lives spiritually, socially, intellectually, and physically. These four areas are interrelated, as are the four tires of an automobile. If one tire is low on air, the other three are adversely affected. If one tire goes completely flat, the other three tires are limited in their ability to function. We perform at our best when we excel in all four areas (spiritual, social, intellectual, and physical).

Living a Balanced Life

"Make sure that you're not so busy making a living that you forget to actually live."
— **Tony Dungy**

The founder and CEO of the multi-billion dollar Hobby Lobby stores has learned the importance of balance, writing, "I tell everyone at Hobby Lobby that...their family is more important than this business. I'm not looking for people who will work seventy or eighty hours a week. If a manager tells me he's so committed to running a perfect store that he's putting in those kind of hours, I tell him to leave. Go somewhere else. I don't care if I'm making all the money in the world from his store—if that's what it takes, I'm not interested. As a matter of fact, that is not what it takes, I know from personal experience. If you're willing to delegate, and you're organized, you don't have to burn the midnight oil very often."[11]

Like the retail industry, professional football is a highly competitive environment where the perception is you have to work extremely long hours to succeed. As a result, many NFL coaches work ridiculously long hours. Former Pittsburgh Steelers head coach Chuck Noll believed in hard work but also believed in having a balanced life. Coach Noll kept reasonable hours for himself and his staff and is living proof that you can have balance and succeed even in a highly competitive environment. With four championships, he holds the record for the most Super Bowl victories by any coach.

Former coach Tony Dungy worked with Chuck Noll for part of his career. He wrote, "Chuck often preached the importance of time away from the office, and we knew it wasn't just lip service. Chuck lived out his message.... His philosophy was, 'Get the work done so you can enjoy the other parts of your life.'... The Steelers organization was certainly a great place for me to learn and to shape a philosophy."[12]

This philosophy was a stark contrast to other NFL teams. While coaching at Kansas City, Coach Dungy sometimes found himself still watching films with the head coach at 3 a.m. Dungy wrote, "After those crazy hours, however, I vowed that if I ever had the chance to make the schedule myself, I wouldn't spend or allow my assistants to spend that much time in the office. With Chuck Noll, I had seen firsthand that it was possible to work fewer hours and still be successful."[13] When Tony Dungy became a head coach, he limited his time in the office and again proved that you can have a balanced life and success in the NFL.

Coach Dungy also emphasized to the players that football was not their highest priority, saying, "I tell our players all the time that even though we put a lot of time and hard work into preparing for games, and as great as it feels to win, they should never let their work come before their families. If they do, I know someday they'll regret it."[14] Coach Dungy set a record for consecutive playoff appearances by a head coach with ten, and won the Super Bowl in 2007.

The great NFL running back Walter Payton recognized that football was only one part of his life. When asked how he wanted to be remembered, he replied, "If all I'm remembered for is a bunch of yards and a lot of touchdowns, I've failed. That was just my work. I want to be remembered as a guy who raised two pretty special kids and who taught them to be great people. Please write that about me. All the honors are great, but personally I would ask that anyone who wants to pay tribute to me, for any reason, I would say there is one thing you can do above everything else and that is: Never let a day go by where you neglect to tell your loved ones that you love them."[15]

"What will people remember us for?... God's definition of success is really one of significance—the significant difference our lives can make in the lives of others. This significance doesn't show up in win-loss records, long resumes, or the trophies gathering dust on our mantels. It's found in the hearts and lives of those we've come across who are in some way better because of the way we lived." [16]

Balancing Work and Family

During my final year in business school, I attended a lecture series held by the Center for Entrepreneurship. Each week a successful entrepreneur was brought in to teach the students and to answer questions they might have. Although meeting with these entrepreneurs was both enjoyable and educational, I was troubled by a pattern that I observed in too many of their lives. Many had allowed their lives to become dominated by their businesses. Although their businesses succeeded, their stories were filled with tragic accounts of broken and lost relationships as a result of neglect. Often, with tears in their eyes, they would warn aspiring entrepreneurs in the room that no success in business can compensate for the loss of family relationships. They would express how they wished they could go back and do things differently. Many expressed their biggest regret as spending too much time at the office and not enough time with family.

Observing this pattern, I began asking the guest entrepreneurs this question: "Could you have done both—built a large business and maintained family relationships?" Most of the entrepreneurs believed they could have done both, and many described the changes they made on future endeavors to maintain a balanced life.

These sad experiences of divorce and strained relationships with children stuck with me. I committed to myself that I would not make these same mistakes with my own family. After graduation, I started a new business with the goal of building a multimillion-dollar enterprise. More importantly, though, I also had the goal to be a good husband, father, minister, and philanthropist. I understood I needed to limit my time in the office to be able to maintain balance. As I built my business, I averaged working thirty-five hours a week. This left me ample time to focus on family and ministry as well. Since I had a young family, I also decided it was vital to limit my travel, so I was on the road for only a couple of days each year. Many were surprised at how little I traveled since most executives in my industry traveled extensively. Since I began with the end in mind, I was able to build a large company while also succeeding as a husband, father, minister, and philanthropist.

Questions to Create Your Mission Statements

On a piece of paper or a computer, answer the following questions and then formulate a rough draft of your mission statements.

What do I deeply enjoy doing?

What four things are most important to me?

What can I do best that would be of worth to others?

What would I like said about me at my funeral?

What things in life make me happy?

How can I help others achieve happiness?

What do I enjoy sharing with others?

What accomplishments am I most excited about?

What problems in my family, community, nation and world most concern me? What can I do to help?

What am I most afraid of for my children? What can I do to help?

If I had one year to live, what would I do?

What stewardships do I currently have? Do they help me fulfill my missions and obtain my dreams? Why or why not?

What stewardships in life will help me fulfill my life's purpose and vision? (i.e., father/mother, husband/wife, student, church member, worker, family member, community leader, writer, teacher, business owner, etc.)

Of the stewardships I have identified, what stewardships will I focus on? (i.e., father/mother, husband/wife, student, church member, worker, family member, community leader, author, teacher, business owner, etc.)

What is my purpose/mission in each stewardship?

Examples of Mission Statements

Role/Stewardship: Personal Renewal and Growth
Mission: To learn, grow, and improve each day.

Role/Stewardship: Father or Mother
Mission: To set a good example for my children. To teach and provide my children opportunities to learn, grow, and achieve their full potential.

Role/Stewardship: Minister
Mission: To bring individuals happiness in this life and eternal life in the world to come.

Role/Stewardship: Employee at Nike
Mission: To bring inspiration and innovation to every athlete in the world.

Role/Stewardship: Author
Mission: Inspire the world to learn and live the principles of success.

Role/Stewardship: Yogurtland Owner
Mission: Provide the finest yogurt and toppings in a clean, fun environment.

"*Twenty years from now you will be more disappointed by the things that you didn't do than by the ones you did do. So throw off the bowlines. Sail away from the safe harbor. Catch the trade winds in your sails. Explore. Dream. Discover.*"

— **Mark Twain**

STEP 3: CREATE YOUR VISION

"Success is determined not so much by the size of one's brain as it is by the size of one's thinking.... Think little goals and expect little achievements. Think big goals and win big success."
— **Dr. David J. Schwartz**

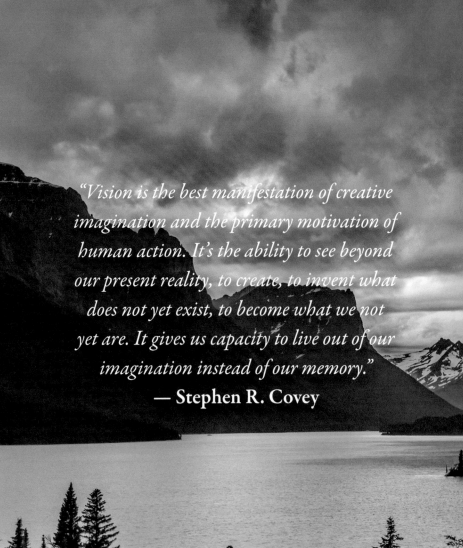

"*Vision is the best manifestation of creative imagination and the primary motivation of human action. It's the ability to see beyond our present reality, to create, to invent what does not yet exist, to become what we not yet are. It gives us capacity to live out of our imagination instead of our memory.*"
— **Stephen R. Covey**

STEP 3
CREATE YOUR VISION

"Viktor Frankl, an Austrian psychologist who survived the death camps of Nazi Germany, made a significant discovery. As he found within himself the capacity to rise above his humiliating circumstances, he became an observer as well as a participant in the experience. He watched others who shared in the ordeal. He was intrigued with the question of what made it possible for some people to survive when most died. He looked at several factors—health, vitality, family structure, intelligence, survival skills. Finally, he concluded that none of these factors was primarily responsible. The single most significant factor, he realized, was a sense of future vision—the impelling conviction of those who were to survive that they had a mission to perform, some important work left to do."[17]

A vision statement will help you clearly define your future desired ends and the direction you wish to go. It will clearly articulate your dreams in such a way that it motivates and inspires you to achieve and live your dreams. It describes what the future will be like. Your vision statement will vividly portray what you want to accomplish and an ideal state of life.

Defining your dreams is the most important thing you can do to get what you want out of life. Dreams provide the motivation to do what it takes to succeed. It is the powerful burning inside that will move you to action. Apathy, laziness, boredom, and low self-esteem result from a lack of vision and purpose. Vision and purpose create enthusiasm, drive, diligence, and dedication to bring forth the dream. Dreams motivate and create action. "Vision is the fundamental force that drives everything else in our lives."[18]

Author Mark Victor Hansen wrote, "You owe it to yourself and humanity to set gigantic, seemingly impossible goals that will help everyone. Whether you have high aim or low aim, you will hit it; if you have low aim, you have no aim at all and will hit nothing. It grieves me to watch individuals squander their lives because they have neglected the process of writing down their personal goals. The process of setting and getting goals is fun."[19]

You are capable of doing great things. "Our deepest fear is not that we are inadequate. Our deepest fear is that we are powerful beyond measure. It is our light, not our darkness that most frightens us. We ask ourselves, Who am I to be brilliant, gorgeous, talented, and fabulous? Actually, who are you not to be? You are a child of God. Your playing small does not serve the world. There is nothing enlightened about shrinking so that other people will not feel insecure around you. We are all meant to shine, as children do. We were born to make manifest the glory of God that is within us. It is not just in some of us; it is in everyone. As we let our own light shine, we unconsciously give others permission to do the same. As we are liberated from our own fear, our presence automatically liberates others."[20] You are to dream big.

Vision Statement Activities

Make your dreams tangible by learning about them. If there is a certain group of people or a cause you would like to help, find out what help they need and what things they are doing to improve people's lives. If there is a particular car you would like to own, learn about it, drive it, and put pictures of the car where you can see them. If you desire a certain vacation, learn about it, get brochures and pictures, and visit web sites about the vacation. Look at different houses and neighborhoods to find out what you like and where you may want to live. If you want to become a successful business owner, read books about it, take classes on it, and learn from people who are where you want to be.

Martin Luther King's Vision Statement

"I have a dream that one day this nation will rise up and live out the true meaning of its creed: 'We hold these truths to be self-evident: that all men are created equal.' I have a dream that one day on the red hills of Georgia the sons of former slaves and the sons of former slave owners will be able to sit down together at the table of brotherhood. I have a dream that one day even the state of Mississippi, a state sweltering with the heat of injustice, sweltering with the heat of oppression, will be transformed into an oasis of freedom and justice. I have a dream that my four little children will one day live in a nation where they will not be judged by the color of their skin but by the content of their character. I have a dream today. I have a dream that one day, down in Alabama, with its vicious racists, with its governor having his lips dripping with the words of interposition and nullification; one day right there in Alabama, little black boys and black girls will be able to join hands with little white boys and white girls as sisters and brothers. I have a dream today. I have a dream that one day every valley shall be exalted, every hill and mountain shall be made low, the rough places will be made plain, and the crooked places will be made straight, and the glory of the Lord shall be revealed, and all flesh shall see it together."

Sample Vision Statement

I am free, happy, and having fun. I have a wonderful family filled with love and joy. I have time every day to spend with my wife and children. My wife is a full-time mother, and I am a full-time father. I own a beautiful home filled with inspirational art, a home theater, and a game room. I have a home in Hawaii, which allows my family and me to experience the beauty, spirit, and peace of the islands. I have several best-selling books, which have sold millions of copies worldwide. I have lectured throughout the world helping millions to learn and live the principles of success. I am debt free and pay cash for everything I do and buy. I have complete financial freedom so I am free to serve God and build His Kingdom. I use the resources I have been blessed with to help others and move forth projects to make the world a better place and help those in need. I take vacations every year with my family and friends. We have gone to Hawaii, Australia, Lake Powell, Orlando, San Diego, Tonga, Samoa, Peru, Alaska, Israel, China, Africa, and the Bahamas. I associate with great men and women, which helps build my faith and love of life. My life is filled with love, peace, happiness, integrity, service, and righteousness.

Questions to Write Your Vision Statement

On a piece of paper or a computer, answer the following questions and then formulate a rough draft of your vision statement.

If I had unlimited time and money, what would I do?

Describe my ideal life. Describe specifics. What would I have? What would I do?

What vacations would I like to take with my family?

Since I become like those with whom I associate, with whom would I like to associate?

Who would I like to help? To what causes would I like to contribute?

How can I make the world a better place?

What would I like to give to family, friends, church, community, and the world?

What standard of living do I want to provide for my family?

What income level would I like to have?

Where would I like to live? Describe my ideal home and surroundings.

What do I deeply enjoy doing?

What recreational activities do I enjoy?

What can I do that would help others?

What do I dream about doing?

What comforts of life would I like to enjoy?

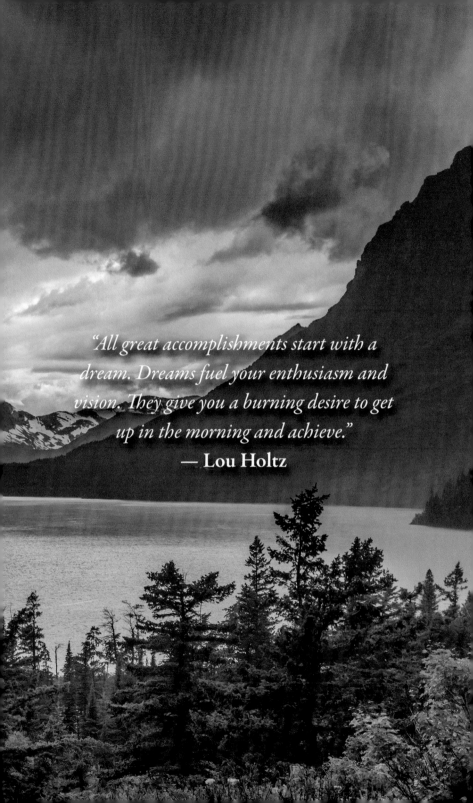

"All great accomplishments start with a dream. Dreams fuel your enthusiasm and vision. They give you a burning desire to get up in the morning and achieve."
— **Lou Holtz**

STEP 4: WRITE DOWN YOUR GOALS

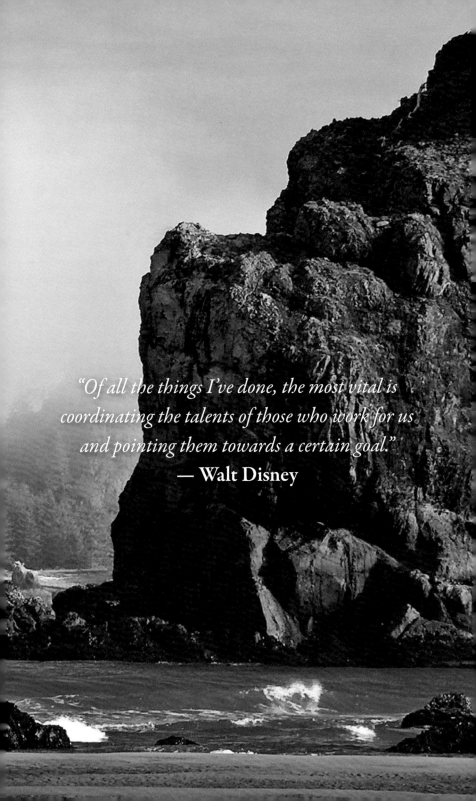

"Of all the things I've done, the most vital is coordinating the talents of those who work for us and pointing them towards a certain goal."
— **Walt Disney**

"You have to have a dream to have a dream come true."
— Bonny Warner, Olympian

STEP 4
WRITE DOWN YOUR GOALS

"Once you know your life purpose, determine your vision, and clarify what your true needs and desires are, you have to convert them into specific, measureable goals and objectives.... Experts on the science of success know the brain is a goal-seeking organism. Whatever goal you give to your subconscious mind, it will work night and day to achieve."[21] It is important to clearly define your values, missions, and vision before you write down your goals. "You don't want to get to the top of the ladder only to find out you had it leaning up against the wrong wall."[22]

Lou Holtz and the Power of Written Goals

Before Coach Lou Holtz was a national champion and member of the College Football Hall of Fame, he struggled to survive as an assistant coach. Coach Holtz wrote of being fired by Paul Dietzel as an assistant at the University of South Carolina: "At least Coach Dietzel offered some words of encouragement. As I was leaving his office after receiving the bad news, he said, 'Lou, just one more thing.'

'Yes?' I said.

'Have you ever thought about going into a different profession?'

"I was twenty-eight years old and had already been through three assistant-coaching jobs in three different states. I'd been rejected for the only head-coaching job I'd applied for, and now I was a couple of months away from being out on the street with nothing.... When it's now or never, everyone tends to focus...I was no different. When I was unemployed...I focused with laser-like intensity on the goals I had for my family and me.... I sat down and reflected on the goals I wanted to achieve in my life. I broke the list down into five categories:

Things I want to do as a husband and a father

Things I want to do religiously

Things I want to accomplish professionally

Things I want to do financially

Things I want to do for excitement (personally)

"When I finished I had 108 items listed. In the 'for excitement' column, I wrote things such as 'jump out of an airplane,' 'land on an aircraft carrier,' 'go out on a submarine,' 'appear on *The Tonight Show* with Johnny Carson,' 'go white-water rafting down the Snake River,' 'play the greatest golf courses in the world,' 'have dinner in the White House,' 'meet the Pope,' 'go on an African picture safari,' and 'run with the bulls in Spain with a slower person.' Forty years later, I've completed all but two of the items from my original list."[23]

Written Goal and Chicken Soup for the Soul

Jack Canfield, who co-authored *Chicken Soup for the Soul* with Mark Victor Hansen, wrote, "When I first started working for W. Clement Stone, he taught me to write my most important goal on the back of my business card and carry it in my wallet at all times. Every time I would open my wallet, I would be reminded of my most important goal. When I met Mark Victor Hansen, I discovered that he, too, used the same technique. After finishing the first *Chicken Soup for the Soul* book, we wrote, 'I am so happy selling 1.5 million copies of *Chicken Soup for the Soul* by Dec. 20, 1994.' We then signed each other's cards and carried them in our wallets. I still have mine in a frame behind my desk. Though our publisher laughed and told us we were crazy, we went on to sell 1.3 million copies of the book by our target date. Some might say, 'Well, you missed your goal by 200,000 copies.' Perhaps, but not by much...and that book went on to sell well over 8 million copies in over 20 languages around the world. Believe me...I can live with that kind of 'failure.'"[24]

Examples of Roles/Stewardships/Missions/Goals

Role/Stewardship: Personal Renewal and Growth

Mission: To learn, grow, and improve each day.

Long-Term Goals: Obtain an MBA, weigh 165 lbs., run a marathon, write a book

Intellectual: Short-Term Goals: Read wisdom literature two hours a week

Spiritual: Short-Term Goals: Daily Bible study and weekly church attendance

Physical: Short-Term Goals: Exercise an hour three times a week

Social: Short-Term Goals: Date night with spouse each week

Role/Stewardship: Father or Mother

Mission: To set a good example for my children. To teach and provide my children opportunities to learn, grow, and achieve their full potential.

Long-Term Goals: Son receive basketball scholarship at university

Short-Term Goals: Practice basketball with son five times a week

Role/Stewardship: Minister

Mission: To bring individuals happiness in this life and eternal life in the world to come.

Long-Term Goals: Learn Greek and Hebrew, congregation of more than 1,000 each Sunday

Short-Term Goals: Take course on ancient Greek, outreach to 2,500 homes surrounding church to invite to Easter services

Role/Stewardship: Employee at Nike

Mission: To bring inspiration and innovation to every athlete in the world.

Long-Term Goals: Become vice president of marketing

Short-Term Goals: Obtain Jackson Ware as client

Role/Stewardship: Author

Mission: Inspire the world to learn and live the principles of success.

Long-Term Goals: Become a best-selling author and sell over one million books

Short-Term Goals: Write one chapter a week, do five things each day to market my books

Role/Stewardship: Yogurtland Owner

Mission: Provide the finest real yogurt and toppings in a clean, fun environment.

Long-Term Goals: Annual revenue of $1 million with $200,000 profit

Short-Term Goals: Do five things each day to market the store

Goals Questions

During my life, what do I want to accomplish in each role?

What one thing could I do in each role that would have the greatest positive impact in accomplishing my mission?

Personal Renewal & Growth Questions

Write down what you can do daily to ensure your growth and renewal spiritually, socially, intellectually, and physically.

What books will I read to help me renew and grow spiritually, socially, intellectually, and physically?

Create Goals for Your Roles/Stewardships

Role/Stewardship:

Mission:

Long-Term Goals:

Short-Term Goals:

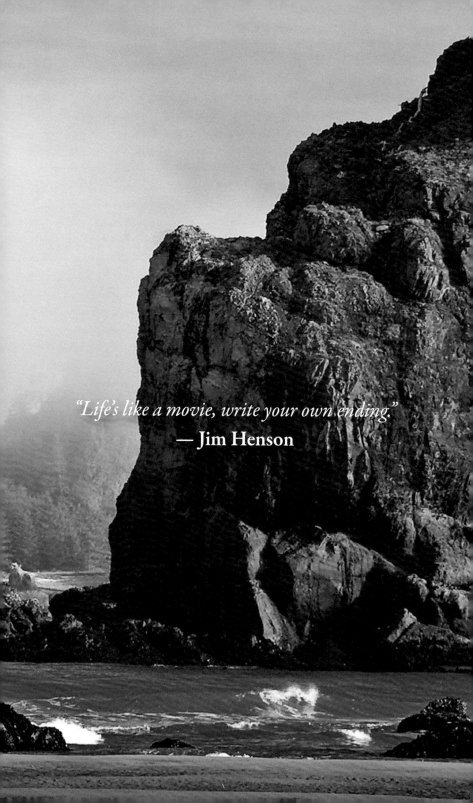

"Life's like a movie, write your own ending."
— Jim Henson

STEP 5: READ YOUR GOALS DAILY

"The truly tough man is the one who stays grounded in his values and focused on his goals when things are challenging."
— **Tony Dungy**

"The number one reason most people don't get what they want is that they don't know what they want."
— T. Harv Eker

STEP 5
READ YOUR GOALS DAILY

It is important for goals to be written so they can be read and reviewed. If our goals are not constantly reviewed, they will be forgotten. Studies have been done to see how much information we remember over time. There are obviously many factors to how much information we remember, but all studies show a large drop-off in information that is retained if it is not reviewed. One study showed the retention of information from a one-hour lecture. The students were tested immediately following the lecture to determine what they learned and remembered. When the students were tested again 24 hours later, 50 to 80 percent of the information known at the end of the lecture had already been forgotten. Finally, the students were tested thirty days following the lecture and only a mere 2 to 3 percent of the information was retained.

Your brain is constantly recording information on a temporary basis, such as scraps of conversations heard or what the person in front of you is wearing. Because the information isn't necessary, and because it doesn't come up again, your brain dumps it all off, along with what was learned in the lecture that you actually do want to hold on to. Reviewing information dramatically increases the retention of the information. When the same thing is repeated, your brain says, "This is important. I will keep that." When you are exposed to the same information repeatedly, it takes less and less time to "activate" the information in your long-term memory and it becomes easier for you to retrieve the information when you need it. Reviewing the information once for ten minutes raised the information retained after 24 hours to over 90 percent.[25]

Keeping your vision, mission, goals, and values at the forefront of your thoughts will greatly enhance the likelihood of their achievement. Doing this will help to keep you focused on living and achieving the life you desire and will guard against them being pushed aside in daily pursuits. You should review your Statement of Excellence at least once a day. "The person who is dedicated and can discipline himself will be the one who succeeds most often."[26]

The words we put into our minds affect our actions. As you constantly review your values and how you want to respond in various situations, when the moments of choice occur throughout the day, your actions are more likely to align with your values and goals.

"*Be careful of your words for your words become your deeds.*"
— **Anonymous**

STEP 6: VISUALIZE

"Look at things not as they are, but as they can be. Visualization adds value to everything. A big thinker always visualizes what can be done in the future. He isn't stuck with the present."
— **Dr. David J. Schwartz**

"We have an amazing ability to accomplish whatever our minds tell us we can do, a phenomenon that has been recognized throughout history."
— Tony Dungy

STEP 6
VISUALIZE

There is great power in the words we put into our minds, but there is even greater power with images. As the old saying goes, "A picture is worth a thousand words." Our written goals create a blueprint for the life we want to build. Visualization enables us to see the finished result. Visualization creates a clear picture of what you want your life to be like. The images we place into our minds affect our actions. As you are faced with choices, you are more likely to do the things that will move you toward the ideal you have visualized.

Many people have been conditioned with thoughts of what can't be done. Studies have shown that within the first eighteen years of our lives, the average person is told "no" more than 148,000 times.[27] We are constantly being told by parents, friends, teachers, television, and co-workers what we cannot do. This conditioning causes many to achieve only a small fraction of their potential. Visualization helps break this conditioning and enables you to see the impossible as accomplished. The regular practice of seeing your vision and goals as reality creates a belief that it can be done. Visualizing your goals daily "will increase your motivation, stimulate your creativity, and heighten your awareness of resources that can help you achieve your goal."[28]

Visualizing the Impossible

In 1952, Roger Bannister set the goal to be the first man to run a mile in under 4 minutes. The record for the mile run remained at 4 minutes and 1.4 seconds for nine years. "For years, the four-minute mile was considered not merely unreachable but, according to physiologists of the time, dangerous to the health of any athlete who attempted to reach it."[29] In an interview, Bannister said, "There was a mystique, a belief that it couldn't be done, but I think it was more of a psychological barrier than a physical barrier."[30] To help break this psychological barrier, Bannister visualized running the race in 3 minutes and 59 seconds. He wrote, "Each night...I ran the race over in my mind."[31] Visualization enabled him to see the goal as possible.

On May 6, 1954, Bannister ran the mile in 3 minutes and 59.4 seconds, setting a new world record and breaking the proclaimed "impossible" barrier. Once Bannister removed this psychological barrier, the door was opened for others to achieve this feat. On June 21, 1954, just forty-six days after Bannister had set the record, John Landy broke Bannister's record in Turku, Finland, and today there are hundreds of people who have run a mile in under four minutes.

The Power of Mental Practice

*"I have always believed, if you want to be a champion,
you will have to win every race in your mind 100 times
before you win it in real life."*
— Marty Liquori, Olympian

"The visualization process can be defined as the conscious creation of mental or sensory images for the purpose of enhancing your life.... [Visualization] is not wishful thinking or daydreaming.... It is a learned skill that requires effort, concentration, discipline, and regular practice.... Inspiring images can create powerful emotions and produce superior performances.... At first you may not fully believe you can perform up to the level of your visualizations. It's okay to act as if it is already happening. With practice your body will come into line with your mental images.... Using imagery or visualization you can create, in vivid detail, a replay of one of your best performances in the past, or you can mentally rehearse an upcoming event, and you can see yourself doing it right.... When you imagine yourself performing an action, you are transmitting electrical impulses to the muscles involved in executing the action."[32]

Former NFL coach Tony Dungy used visualization with his teams. He wrote, "All football teams rely on visualization to increase their chances of success.... The first thing you have to do when you're trying to turn a football franchise from a loser to a winner is to create the belief that you can win. Most of the time the talent is already there to accomplish great things, but there is no belief that it will happen. Our minds are powerful instruments and should not be taken lightly.... You will never be able to rise above the imaginary ceiling you construct in your mind."[33]

Olympic sprinter Valerie Brisco-Hooks used the power of visualization to assist in achieving her goals. Her coach, Bobby Kersee, challenged her to set a goal for the 400-meter race at the National Championships in San Jose. Valerie set the goal to become the first American woman to run the 400 meter in under 50 seconds. As a part of her training and workouts, Valerie's coach had her visualize every part of the race. At the National Championships she won the race with a new American record, covering the distance in 49.89 seconds.[34] Valerie went on to win three gold medals at the 1984 Olympics.

Mental Practice Study

"Harvard University researchers found that students who visualized in advance performed tasks with nearly 100% accuracy, whereas students who didn't visualize achieved only 55% accuracy.... Visualization—or the art of creating compelling and vivid pictures in your mind—may be the most underutilized success tool you possess."[35]

Visualize the Positive

"Old minds are like old horses; you must exercise them
if you wish to keep them in working order."
— **John Adams**

Visualization can lift our performance, but it can also hurt our performance if we visualize the negative. I ran the hurdles in high school and my natural tendency before a race was to see myself hitting a hurdle, falling down, and everyone laughing. I had to fight this tendency as I prepared for a race. When these negative thoughts would enter my mind, I would quickly remove them and replace them with positive images of running a perfect race.

There is a natural tendency to visualize the negative. For example, before a big test you may think to yourself, "I am going to do poorly," or, "I am not going to remember the information." You must transform these thoughts to visualize the positive and see yourself scoring well on the exam and remembering the answers. You must guard against negative mental practice since it will hurt performance.

Create Images of Your Goals

To create an image of his goal of running a mile under 4 minutes, Roger Bannister had a photo taken of himself crossing the finish line at the end of a mile race. On the photo, he wrote the time of 3:59. When I set the goal to do a million dollars of business in a month, I purchased a pure silver, gold-plated million-dollar bill from the U.S. Mint. I placed the million-dollar bill in my office where I would see it regularly as a reminder of the goal. My oldest son has set several goals, and we created a poster board he keeps in his bedroom with images representing his goals. One of his goals is to attend a university, so we got images of the university, pasted them to the board, and wrote his goal next to the images. Another one of his goals was to go deep sea fishing, so we found images of deep sea fishing and placed them on the poster board. He now has visual images to remind him of his goals. I recommend placing images of your goals in prominent places such as your bathroom mirror, the refrigerator, the headboard of your bed, and the dashboard of your car. Keeping your goals at the forefront of your thoughts will greatly enhance your likelihood of achieving them.

Visualization Becoming Reality

Olympic gold medalist Peter Vidmar shares how he used visualization as a part of his training routine:

To keep us focused on our Olympic goal, we began ending our workouts by visualizing our dream. We visualized ourselves actually competing in the Olympics and achieving our dream by practicing what we thought would be the ultimate gymnastics scenario.

I'd say, "Okay, Tim, let's imagine it's the men's gymnastics finals of the Olympic Games. The United States team is on its last event of the night, which just happens to be the high bar. The last two guys up for the United States are Tim Daggett and Peter Vidmar. Our team is neck and neck with the People's Republic of China, the reigning world champions, and we have to perform our routines perfectly to win the Olympic team gold medal."

At that point we'd each be thinking, "Yeah, right. We're never going to be neck and neck with those guys. They were number one at the Budapest world championships while our team didn't even win a medal. It's never going to happen." But what if it did happen? How would we feel?

We'd close our eyes and, in this empty gym at the end of a long day, we'd visualize an Olympic arena with 13,000 people in the seats and another 200 million watching live on television. Then we'd practice our routines. First, I'd be the announcer. I'd cup my hands around my mouth and say, "Next up, from the United States of America, Tim Daggett." Then Tim would go through his routine as if it were the real thing.

Then Tim would go over to the corner of the gym, cup his hands around his mouth, and, in his best announcer voice, say, "Next up, from the United States of America, Peter Vidmar."

Then it was my turn. In my mind, I had one chance to perfectly perform my routine in order for our team to win the gold medal. If I didn't, we'd lose.

Tim would shout out, "Green light," and I'd look at the superior judge, who was usually our Coach Mako. I'd raise my hand, and he'd raise his right back. Then I'd turn, face the bar, grab hold, and begin my routine.

Well, a funny thing happened on July 31, 1984. It was the Olympic Games, men's gymnastics team finals in Pauley Pavilion on the UCLA campus. The 13,000 seats were all filled, and a television audience in excess of 200 million around the world tuned in. The United States team was on its last event of the night, the high bar. The last two guys up for the United States just happened to be Tim Daggett and Peter Vidmar. And just as we visualized, our team was neck and neck with the People's Republic of China. We had to perform our high bar routines perfectly to win the gold medal.

I looked at Coach Mako, my coach for the past 12 years. As focused as ever, he simply said, "Okay, Peter, let's go. You know what to do. You've done it a thousand times, just like every day back in the gym. Let's just do it one more time, and let's go home. You're prepared."

He was right. I had planned for this moment and visualized it hundreds of times. I was prepared to perform my routine. Rather than seeing myself actually standing in the Olympic arena with 13,000 people in the stands and 200 million watching on television, in my mind I pictured myself back in the UCLA gym at the end of the day with two people left in the gym.

When the announcer said, "From the United States of America, Peter Vidmar," I imagined it was my buddy Tim Daggett saying it. When the green light came on, indicating it was time for the routine, I imagined that it wasn't really a green light but that it was Tim shouting, "Green light!" And when I raised my hand toward the superior judge from East Germany, in my mind I was signaling my coach, just like I had signaled him every day at the end of hundreds of workouts. In the gym, I always visualized I was at the Olympic finals; at the Olympic finals, I visualized I was back in the gym.

I turned, faced the bar, jumped up, and grabbed on. I began the same routine I had visualized and practiced day after day in the gym. I was in memory mode, going yet again where I'd already gone hundreds of times.

I quickly made it past the risky double-release move that had harpooned my chances at the world championships. I moved smoothly through the rest of my routine and landed a solid dismount, where I anxiously waited for my score from the judges.

With a deep voice the announcement came through the speaker, "The score for Peter Vidmar is 9.95." "Yes!" I shouted. "I did it!" The crowd cheered loudly as my teammates and I celebrated our victory.

Thirty minutes later, we were standing on the Olympic medal platform in the Olympic arena with 13,000 people in the stands and over 200 million watching on television, while the gold medals were officially draped around our necks. Tim, me, and our teammates stood proudly wearing our gold medals as the national anthem played and the American flag was raised to the top of the arena. It was a moment we visualized and practiced hundreds of times in the gym. Only this time, it was for real.

"Imagination is everything. It is the preview of life's coming attractions."
— **Albert Einstein**

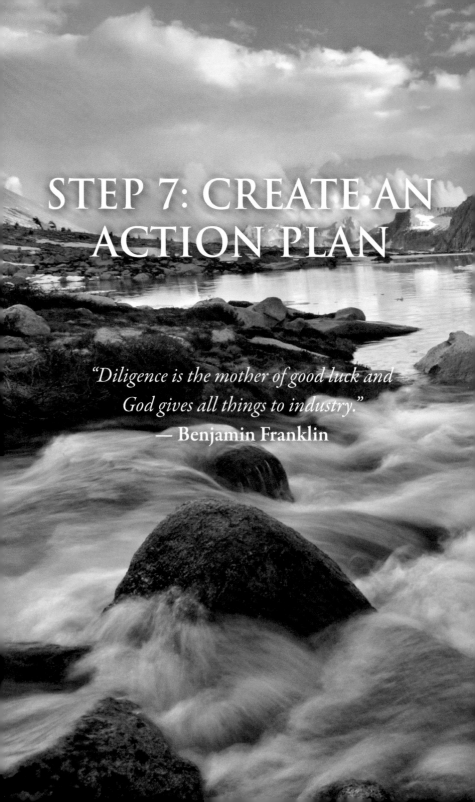

STEP 7: CREATE AN ACTION PLAN

*"Diligence is the mother of good luck and
God gives all things to industry."*
— Benjamin Franklin

"*Winning is never accidental. All successful coaches and players have at least one thing in common: a strong game plan. They had clearly defined goals and consistent work habits.*"
— Lou Holtz

STEP 7
CREATE AN ACTION PLAN

You can write and visualize goals all you want, but if you do not take action, your goals will never become a reality. To obtain a goal you have never before achieved will require tasks you have never before done.

The Ten-Thousand-Hour Rule

"Practice isn't the thing you do once you're good. It's the thing you do that makes you good.... In fact, researchers have settled on what they believe is the magic number for true expertise: ten thousand hours."[36]

Dr. Daniel Levitin writes, "Ten thousand hours of practice is required to achieve the level of mastery associated with being a world-class expert—in anything. In study after study, of composers, basketball players, fiction writers, ice skaters, concert pianists, chess players, master criminals, and what have you, this number comes up again and again. Ten thousand hours is the equivalent to roughly three hours per day, or twenty hours per week, of practice over ten years.... No one has yet found a case in which true world-class expertise was accomplished in less time. It seems that it takes the brain this long to assimilate all that it needs to know to achieve true mastery."[37]

Benjamin Franklin's Action Plan

After Benjamin Franklin wrote down the thirteen virtues he wanted to live by, he created an action plan to have them be more than just idle words on a page or a mere wish to be accomplished. Benjamin Franklin described the process of reviewing and working to develop each of these virtues. He wrote in his autobiography, "My intention being to acquire the habitude of all these virtues, I judged it would be well not to distract my attention by attempting the whole at once, but to fix one of them at a time.... I made a little book, in which I allotted a page for each of the virtues. I ruled each page with red ink, so as to have seven columns, one for each day of the week, marking each column with a letter for the day. I crossed these columns with thirteen red lines, marking the beginning of each line with the first letter of one of the virtues, on which line, and in its proper column, I might mark, by a little black spot, every fault I found upon examination to have been committed respecting that virtue upon that day. I determined to give a week's strict attention to each of the virtues successively.

"Thus, in the first week, my great guard was to avoid the least offence against Temperance, leaving the other virtues to their ordinary chance, only marking every evening the faults of the day. Thus, if in the first week I could keep my first line, marked T, clear of spots, I supposed the habit of that virtue so much strengthened and its opposite weakened, that I might venture extending my attention to include the next, and for the following week keep both lines clear of spots. Proceeding thus to the last, I could go through a course complete in thirteen weeks, and four courses in a year. And like him who, having a garden to weed, does not attempt to eradicate all the bad herbs at once, which would exceed his reach and his strength, but works on one of the beds at a time, and, having accomplished the first, proceeds to a second, so I should have, I hoped, the encouraging pleasure of seeing on my pages the progress I made in virtue."[38] An action plan is necessary for your values to become your virtues.

Philo T. Farnsworth's Action Plan

Before Philo "Phil" T. Farnsworth was a famous inventor with three hundred patents, he was a young boy fascinated by the automobile and the electric light bulb. He began to study Henry Ford, Thomas Edison, and other inventors and decided he wanted to be an inventor. He discovered that one of his life missions was to make the world a better place through invention and innovation. He began looking for opportunities and discovered that many people were trying to transmit pictures. Radio was very successful and rapidly growing and improving, but little success was being had on discovering a way to transmit pictures. Phil saw his opportunity and set a goal to create a way to transmit pictures like radio transmitted sound. He created a clear vision for television and began working to make this vision a reality.

Phil persisted for five years before he secured funding to begin developing his invention. Farnsworth's plan to create television would require $25,000 (approximately $325,000 in today's dollars) and a year of work. As soon as Phil secured the funding, he sent for his friend and brother-in-law, Cliff Gardner, to come and work with him in San Francisco. As Phil arrived outside the 600-square-foot room that would become their lab, he said to Cliff, "Behold the future home of electronic television."[39]

Phil's wife, Pem, said of his vision and the beginning day at the San Francisco lab: "[Phil] feared he was still lacking in the experience necessary to complete the monumental task before him. But I knew that the immense energy of his vision would save him from giving up in the face of whatever pitfalls and discouragements lay ahead.... There was nothing that could stand between him and his goal."[40]

Phil began working at an intense pace. The lab journals show that he worked twelve hours a day, six days a week. However, Phil did not work on Sundays to observe the Sabbath Day. Farnsworth created a year plan with a systematic process to create, test, and perfect each of the components needed, with a final test of the entire system working together. The journals showed how he tried one technique after another, documenting what was learned from each attempt and failure. Phil described his work in the lab to Pem on one occasion saying, "I'm a professional mistake maker."

After a year of intense work, they were ready for the first test of the entire television system. This test occurred on September 7, 1927. As the image appeared on the picture field, Farnsworth shouted with excitement, "That's it, folks! We've done it. There you have electronic television."

"The difficult we do right away;
the impossible takes slightly longer."
— **Philo T. Farnsworth**

Wright Brothers' Action Plan

The Wright Brothers' story reveals an action plan and a great deal of work to make their dreams a reality. In 1899, they began their flight experiments. Over the next four years, the Wright Brothers performed thousands of tests, experiments, and flights. In 1901, they created the world's first wind tunnel and tested over two hundred different wing shapes.[41] Just in the months of September and October, 1902, they made over seven hundred fifty glides.[42] After four years of work, on December 17, 1903, Orville, age thirty-two, and Wilbur, age thirty-six, achieved their dream of a controlled, powered flight.

Walt Disney's Action Plan

Walt Disney set a goal to create the first successful full-length animated feature film. His goal was viewed as foolish by those in the movie industry. Even Walt's wife, Lilly, and his brother, Roy, tried to talk him out of his dream. Walt would not let the doubts and opinions of others deter him from his goal, and he began work on the project. Walt met with his top animators and set the vision for the feature film. By the time *Snow White* was completed, the studio had employed more than seven hundred fifty animation craftsmen who created an estimated two million drawings.[43] The film took three years and $1.5 million ($21 million in today's dollars) to create. Walt Disney was not afraid to dream big. Walt's oldest grandson, Chris Miller, said of Walt, "My grandfather had big dreams and goals...and he persevered until he achieved them.... His life teaches all of us to believe in our dreams, to be daring in the pursuit of our goals, and to never back away from a challenge."[44]

Conclusion

"If you are clear where you are going (goals) and you take several steps in that direction every day, you eventually have to get there.... So decide what you want, write it down, review it constantly, and each day do something that moves you toward those goals."[45]

"*Character cannot be developed in ease and quiet. Only through experience of trial and suffering can the soul be strengthened, vision cleared, ambition inspired, and success achieved.*"
— **Helen Keller**

STEP 8:
PERSISTENCE

*"Only those who dare to fail greatly
can ever achieve greatly."*
— Robert F. Kennedy

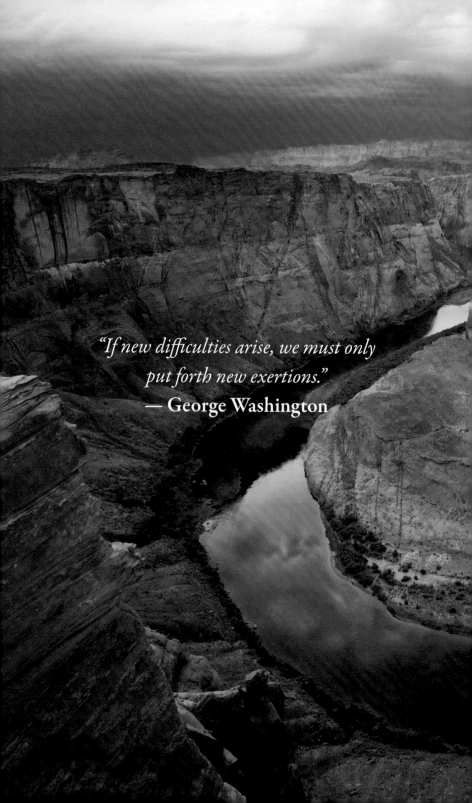

"*If new difficulties arise, we must only put forth new exertions.*"
— **George Washington**

STEP 8
PERSISTENCE

"It's necessary to fail. That's how we learn."
— **Peter Vidmar, Olympian**

"If you're going to chase meaningful dreams and do significant things, you have to be willing to come up short sometimes.... Failure...is a constant in the human experience.... The more I learned about those people I admired for their successes, the more I also began to admire them for the way they handled failures. Success is really a journey of persistence and perseverance in spite of failure."[46]

The Eighth-String Quarterback

Before Steve Young became the MVP of Super Bowl XXIX and a member of the NFL Hall of Fame, he was "a shy, scared boy who refused to go to the second grade without his mother. When growing up, he used to think of excuses why he couldn't go on overnight camping trips because he was afraid to leave home. [Young said], 'I could lie to you and say I was macho, but I wasn't. The most traumatic experience of my life was getting on the airplane and going to college.'"[47]

When Young arrived at Brigham Young University, he did not unpack his bags and called home almost every night.

He missed his family and the familiar surround of his home in Connecticut. Young went to BYU to play football. He played as an option quarterback in high school and earned all-state honors, but he soon found out it was going to be tough to get playing time at BYU. The starting quarterback was Jim McMahon who broke seventy-five NCAA records while at BYU, and there were several quarterbacks competing for the backup roles.

During one of Young's first practices at BYU, the offensive coordinator had each quarterback do a three step drop— something Young had never done before. Young had very little experience throwing the football since he ran the wish bone offense in high school. As Young took the snap, he slipped and landed flat on his butt and fumbled the ball. His teammates laughed and the coach rolled his eyes. Young recalled the coach telling him, "You'll never play quarterback at BYU."

In the locker room, the coaches taped to the wall a depth chart for each position. Young scanned the list of quarterbacks to the eighth and final spot before he found his name, and the offensive coordinator suggested to the head coach that Young be moved to play as a defensive back or safety.

"With seven other quarterbacks ahead of him...it looked hopeless. Heartsick for home, one night he called home and told Grit [his father] he'd had it, he wanted to quit. Grit then gave him some advice which has stuck with Young the rest of his life. 'You can quit if you want to. But you can't come home. This is not a place for a quitter.' Young decided to stay, gut it out, and compete. Although still homesick, he buckled down for the long haul."[48]

When the first game arrived in September, Young headed to the locker room to get ready for the game but found no jersey in his locker. He had not made the cut to dress for the game, so he went as a spectator.

At the next practice following the game, Young was the first one to arrive and the last one to leave. He followed this routine for the rest of the season. Young was moved to practice with the defense, but he continued to work on his skills as a quarterback. He watched film, practiced his drop back moves, learned from the other quarterbacks, and completed various passing drills. In the months of January and February, he threw over 10,000 spirals after practice and his arm ached. "He did everything he could to get better and gain an edge over the competition."[49]

The offensive coordinator, who suggested moving Young to defense, took a head coaching job at San Diego State and the quarterback coach became the new offensive coordinator. The new offensive coordinator had watched Young at practice and really liked what he saw. He had Young moved back to practice with the offense as quarterback, and Young continued to work hard and compete.

At the start of his sophomore year, Young had moved from the eighth-string quarterback to the backup quarterback to Jim

McMahon. In just twelve months, Young had overcome many challenges and convinced many doubters that he could be a starting quarterback. In the fourth game of the season, McMahon went out with an injury and Young got his opportunity to play. He would also start the next two games until McMahon returned from injury. Young vomited before each game as a result of pregame nerves and regularly vomited before games throughout his career.

"Although his performances on the field had been brief, he'd shown enough to start himself on a course that would change his life forever. The stage was set for his junior year.... As the BYU starter his junior year, he completed 230 of 367 passes (a whopping 62 percent) for 3,507 yards while running for 407 more."[50]

During his senior year, Young had a tremendous season, leading the team to an 11-1 record, a national ranking, and a conference championship. Young set the NCAA record for the highest pass completion percentage in a season, completing 71.3 percent of his passes. Young also finished second in voting for the Heisman Trophy. In 1984, at age 22, Young signed a contract worth $40.1 million with the Los Angeles Express of the USFL. Even though he had signed the largest contract in pro sports history, he continued to drive his 1965 Oldsmobile until it died at 270,000 miles.

Steve Young gave this definition of success. "To dream and

strive for those dreams. To enjoy victory and grow stronger with defeat. To live to the fullest and fill other lives with joy. That is success.... To me, the challenges in life are what make it exciting. Half the fun of life is being insecure, wondering if you can make it. The fun is in the earning of your achievement."[51]

Conclusion

The author of the book *Good to Great* conducted an extensive five-year research project to identify the factors that caused companies to create lasting excellence. One of the critical factors identified was perseverance. Jim Collins wrote, "The good-to-great companies faced just as much adversity as the comparison companies, but responded to the adversity differently. They hit the realities of their situation head on. As a result, they emerged from adversity even stronger."[52] Failure is a part of learning, so don't be afraid to fail. The formula for success is to try until you succeed. There are no failures in life, only those who quit before success.

"Many of life's failures are people who did not realize how close they were to success when they gave up."
— *Thomas A. Edison*

CREATING YOUR STATEMENT OF EXCELLENCE

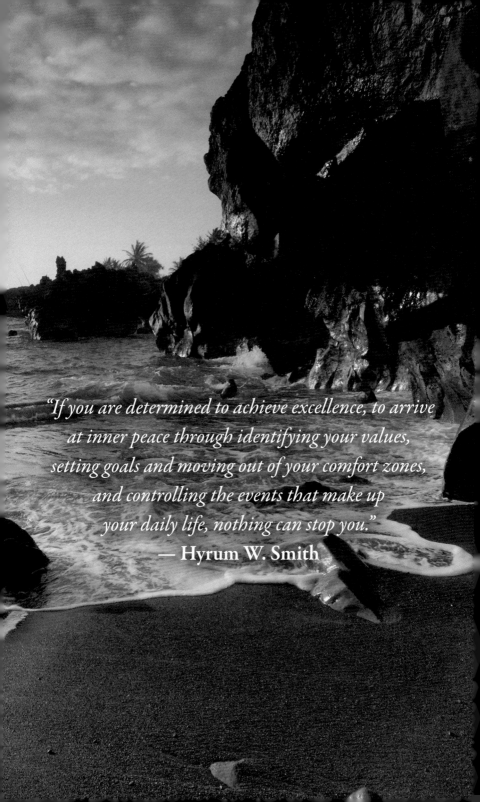

"If you are determined to achieve excellence, to arrive at inner peace through identifying your values, setting goals and moving out of your comfort zones, and controlling the events that make up your daily life, nothing can stop you."
— Hyrum W. Smith

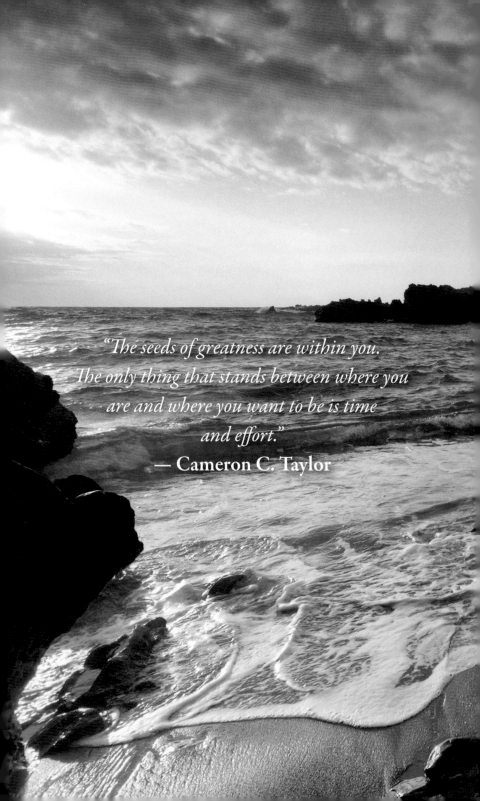

"The seeds of greatness are within you. The only thing that stands between where you are and where you want to be is time and effort."
— **Cameron C. Taylor**

CREATING YOUR STATEMENT OF EXCELLENCE

It is now time to finalize your Statement of Excellence. Using your answers from each of the previous sections, create your Statement of Excellence. Your statement will begin with your values and a description of what each value means to you. Next will be your life roles/stewardships and your mission and goals within each role. The last piece will be your Vision Statement, which vividly portrays what you want to accomplish and your ideal life. Once your Statement of Excellence is completed, the 8 Steps to Lasting Excellence change slightly.

8 Steps to Lasting Excellence

Step 1: Live Your Values

Step 2: Fulfill Your Missions

Step 3: Make Your Vision a Reality

Step 4: Write Down Your Goals

Step 5: Read Your Statement of Excellence Daily

Step 6: Visualize Your Goals and Dreams

Step 7: Create and Execute Your Action Plans

Step 8: Persistence

ABOUT THE AUTHOR

Cameron C. Taylor is a best-selling author, highly sought-after speaker, and entrepreneur. Cameron is the author of the books *Preserve, Protect, and Defend; Does Your Bag Have Holes? 24 Truths That Lead to Financial and Spiritual Freedom; 8 Attributes of Great Achievers;* and *Twelve Paradoxes of the Gospel.* Cameron graduated with honors from business school and is the founder of several successful companies and charities. He is a founder of The Glorious Cause of America Institute and serves on its board of directors. Cameron is a recipient of the *Circle of Honor Award* for being an "exceptional example of honor, integrity, and commitment." He lives in Idaho with his wife and children. Cameron is a gifted teacher who has been invited to speak at hundreds of meetings with excellent reviews.

Cameron's books and lectures have been endorsed by Ken Blanchard, co-author of *The One Minute Manager*; Dr. Stephen R. Covey, author of *The Seven Habits of Highly Effective People*; Billionaire Jon Huntsman, Sr.; Rich DeVos, owner of the Orlando Magic; William Danko, PhD, co-author of *The Millionaire Next Door*; and many others.

"The biggest men and women with the biggest ideas can be shot down by the smallest men and women with the smallest minds.
Think big anyway."
— **Dr. Kent M. Keith**

ENDNOTES

1 Jim Collins, *Good to Great* (New York: HarperCollins, 2001), 164-165.

2 John Wooden with Steve Jamison, *Wooden: A Lifetime of Observations and Reflections On and Off the Court* (New York: McGraw-Hill, 1997), 191.

3 Tony Dungy and Nathan Whitaker, *Quiet Strength* (Carol Stream, IL: Tyndale House Publishers, 2008), 105.

4 Anthony Robbins, *Unlimited Power* (New York: Fireside, 1997), 113–114.

5 Roy Disney, son of Walt Disney.

6 Paul Allen, *Idea Man* (New York: Penguin Group, 1991), 31-32.

7 Don Soderquist, *Live Learn Lead to Make a Difference* (Nashville, TN: J. Countryman, 2006), 121.

8 Viktor Frankl, *Man's Search for Meaning* (Boston, MA: Beacon Press, 1959), 113.

9 Stephen R. Covey, *The Seven Habits of Highly Effective People* (New York: Simon & Schuster, 2004), 128-29.

10 Laurie Beth Jones, *The Path* (New York, NY: Hyperion, 1996), 26.

11 David Green, *More Than a Hobby* (Nashville, TN: Thomas Nelson, 2005), 138-139.

12 Tony Dungy and Nathan Whitaker, *Quiet Strength* (Carol Stream, IL: Tyndale House Publishers, 2008), 58.

13 Tony Dungy and Nathan Whitaker, *Quiet Strength* (Carol Stream, IL: Tyndale House Publishers, 2008), 76.

14 Tony Dungy and Nathan Whitaker, *Quiet Strength* (Carol Stream, IL: Tyndale House Publishers, 2008), 153.

15 Walter Payton, *Never Die Easy* (New York: Villard Books, 2000), 249.

16 Tony Dungy and Nathan Whitaker, *Quiet Strength* (Carol Stream, IL: Tyndale House Publishers, 2008), 144.

17 Stephen R. Covey, A. Roger Merrill, Rebecca R. Merrill, *First Things First* (New York: Simon & Schuster, 1994), 103.

18 Stephen R. Covey, A. Roger Merrill, Rebecca R. Merrill, *First Things First* (New York: Simon & Schuster, 1994), 116.

19 Mark Victor Hansen, *The Future Diary* (Newport Beach: Mark Victor Hansen Publishing Company, 1996), 43.

20 Marianne Williamson, *A Return to Love* (New York: HarperCollins, 1992), 190-191.

21 Jack Canfield, *The Success Principles* (New York: HarperCollins, 2005), 51.

22 Jack Canfield, *The Success Principles* (New York: HarperCollins, 2005), 21.

23 Lou Holtz, *Wins, Losses, and Lessons* (New York: HarperCollins, 2006), 68-70, 74.

24 Jack Canfield, *The Success Principles* (New York: HarperCollins, 2005), 55-56.

25 Retrieved July 17, 2014 from http://uwaterloo.ca/counselling-services/curve-forgetting.

26 Tony Dungy and Nathan Whitaker, *Uncommon* (Carol Stream, IL: Tyndale, 2009), 249.

27 Shad Helmstetter, *What to Say When You Talk to Your Self* (New York: Pocket Books, 1986), 20.

28 Jack Canfield, *The Success Principles* (New York: HarperCollins, 2005), 55.

29 Bruce Lowitt, "Bannister Stuns World with 4-Minute Mile," *St. Petersburg Times*, December 17, 1999.

30 David M. Ewalt and Lacey Rose, "The Greatest Individual Athletic Achievements," *Forbes*, January 29, 2008.

31 Roger Bannister, *The Four-Minute Mile* (Guilford, CT: The Globe Pequot Press, 1981), 207.

32 JoAnn Dahlkoetter, *Olympic Thinking* (JoAnn Dahlkoetter, 2012).

33 Tony Dungy and Nathan Whitaker, *Uncommon* (Carol Stream, IL: Tyndale, 2009), 104, 108.

34 John Naber, *Awaken the Olympian Within* (Torrance, CA: Griffin Publishing Group, 1999), 197.

35 Jack Canfield, *The Success Principles* (New York: HarperCollins, 2005), 81.

36 Malcolm Gladwell, *Outliers* (New York: Little, Brown, and Company, 2008), 42, 40.

37 Daniel J. Levitin, *This is Your Brain on Music* (New York: Penguin Group, 2006), 197.

38 Benjamin Franklin, *The Autobiography of Benjamin Franklin* (Philadelphia: Henry Altemus, 1895), 150-154.

39 Elma G. Farnsworth, *Distant Vision* (Salt Lake City, UT: PemberlyKent Publishers, 1990), 68.

[40] Elma G. Farnsworth, *Distant Vision* (Salt Lake City, UT: PemberlyKent Publishers, 1990), 68.

[41] *Academic American Encyclopedia* (Princeton, NJ: Arete Publishing Co., 1980), 212.

[42] "Wright Brothers", *Wikipedia*. Retrieved December 7, 2006, from http://en.wikipedia.org/wiki/Wright_brothers.

[43] Pat Williams, Jim Denney, *How to Be Like Walt* (Deerfield Beach, FL: HCI, 2004), 120.

[44] Pat Williams, Jim Denney, *How to Be Like Walt* (Deerfield Beach, FL: HCI, 2004), 124.

[45] Jack Canfield, *The Success Principles* (New York: HarperCollins, 2005), 61.

[46] Tony Dungy and Nathan Whitaker, *Uncommon* (Carol Stream, IL: Tyndale, 2009), 137-138.

[47] Dick Harman, *Steve Young: Staying in the Pocket* (Salt Lake City, UT: Black Moon Publishing, 1995), 16.

[48] Dick Harman, *Steve Young: Staying in the Pocket* (Salt Lake City, UT: Black Moon Publishing, 1995), 28.

[49] Dick Harman, *Steve Young: Staying in the Pocket* (Salt Lake City, UT: Black Moon Publishing, 1995), 31.

[50] Dick Harman, *Steve Young: Staying in the Pocket* (Salt Lake City, UT: Black Moon Publishing, 1995), 34-35.

[51] Dick Harman, *Steve Young: Staying in the Pocket* (Salt Lake City, UT: Black Moon Publishing, 1995), 23, 69.

[52] Jim Collins, *Good to Great* (New York: HarperCollins, 2001), 88.

[53] From address "Duties of the Citizen" by Theodore Roosevelt on April 23, 1910 before the French Academy. *The Independent, Volume 68* (1910), 893.

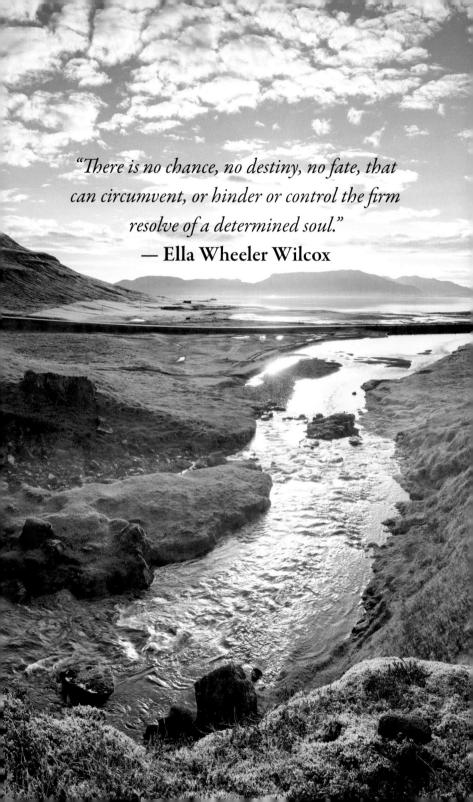

"There is no chance, no destiny, no fate, that can circumvent, or hinder or control the firm resolve of a determined soul."
— Ella Wheeler Wilcox

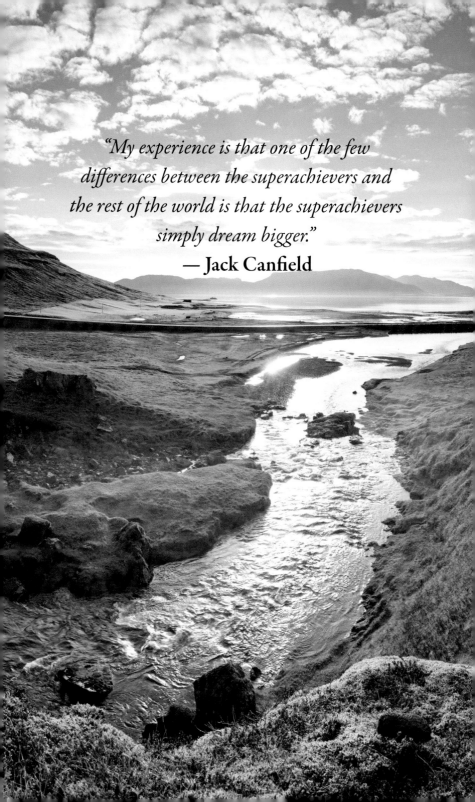

"*My experience is that one of the few differences between the superachievers and the rest of the world is that the superachievers simply dream bigger.*"
— Jack Canfield

"It is not the critic who counts; not the man who points out how the strong man stumbles or where the doer of deeds could have done them better. The credit belongs to the man who is actually in the arena, whose face is marred by dust and sweat and blood; who strives valiantly; who errs, and comes short again and again, because there is no effort without error and shortcoming; but who does actually strive to do the deeds; who knows great enthusiasms, the great devotions; who spends himself in a worthy cause; who at the best knows in the end the triumph of high achievement, and who at the worst, if he fails, at least fails while daring greatly, so that his place shall never be with those cold and timid souls who know neither victory nor defeat."[53]

— **Theodore Roosevelt**